I0570321

EMPOWERMENT 23:

THE WHEELS OF LIFE

ROXIE BERRY

Copyright © 2023 Roxie Berry. All rights reserved. No part of this publication may be reproduced, distributed, or transmitted in any form or by any means, including photocopying, recording, or other electronic or mechanical methods, without the prior written permission of the publisher, except in the case of brief quotations embodied in critical reviews and certain other noncommercial uses permitted by copyright law. For permission requests, write to the publisher, addressed "Attention: Permissions Coordinator," at the address below.

ISBN: 979-8-9902680-4-3

Publishing By: DemiCo National, LLC

www.DemiCoNational.com

Salute

Salute to Sgt. Samuel Jackson Berry, my father who served in the United States Army. My name is Roxie Berry, and my story began in Bessemer Alabama, where I was born and raised. I am the first child born to Roxie and Samuel Berry. The only thing a child thinks about is playing freeze tag, hopscotch, hide and seek, hula hooping, jump ropes, and swinging on the swing set with their friends. A smile from ear to ear formed on my face as family and friends came to visit from out of town, making the day brighter. I was happy as can be. The center gives free lunch and I always tried to get more than one. As skinny as I am, a girl knows how to eat. You would wonder if all the food was going to my brain. On my bicycle, riding up and down the street, just being a carefree child. Ok, let me say it, a tomboy. Climbing the apple trees and catching crayfish. What girls enjoy being ditches? Only Roxie! Getting all dirty while running the street from sunup to sundown. On the summer night of July 20, 1989, everything turned into a nightmare of horror. My father was shot in the front yard of his home as I watched. I was just 12 years old. I fell in a state of disbelief while watching my father die. My world turned into an ongoing nightmare of Daddy issues. The lack of self-confidence, self- doubt, insecurity, self - esteem, self- worth, and self-respect that came from this changed my childhood forever. Her universe was demolished to shred no more hearing I Love You.

Beauty

The saying goes "beauty is skin deep". Beauty is supposed to reflect what is on the inside of your temple, and still, that isn't enough to be satisfied with the thought of being appreciated. It seems like more isn't enough, and enough isn't more. The best of both worlds was no more than the loss of a final touch. Seasons change whether real or fake throughout the course of time. The look in your eyes is such allure as if it was a shade of many colors. Imagine falling deeply for your charisma only to be saddened that you're not the person you're supposed to be. The personality was so natural to go deeper within the mindset of protecting a powerful woman.

The Fighter 4

I remember riding in the limousine to my graduation to receive my associate degree in human services from Midlands Technical College. After 17 long years of hard work, I overcame the challenges that were in my way. Who is my fan club you ask, my children, the Fighter 4. They act like my daddy often telling me what to do. Without them, there would be no me. They had the biggest smiles on their faces as I walked across the stage. Reality set in fast, and the real work began. I felt like I was going on 18 again; trying to find my passion and purpose. Working in a cafeteria and just being the lunch lady was familiar. However, with this new degree, I had to become uncomfortable. Stepping into unknown waters will get you out of your comfort zone and that's okay.

Reaqwon 23

Why didn't you tell me you wanted to leave? I try to hide my pain by masking the depression with a smile. I work hard so that I can cope with being in a world without you. Is it difficult going, seconds, minutes, hours, and even days at a time without hearing your voice? How can a mother bear this? I miss your voice and your hugs. While pregnant with you almost every day I thought about how ugly of a mother I would be. Looking into your eyes the day you were born it was instantly love at first sight. Your small hands smelt so fresh after you made your way from my womb and through the birth canal. Your body was so small, but all small things have to grow at some point. You made your mother become this beautiful woman as rose petals drop one by one on the golden road of redemption. When I got the phone call all I could think about was the path I created for you; it was filled with errors. You will always be my precious child even in Heaven. This experience gave me PTSD...

The Mirror

What is forbidden can't be hidden, especially in plain sight. Something you want but can't have can be a person, place, or thing. Sometimes, what you want isn't good for your mental health. Love is one thing you can't bury or hide from. Love can cause hurt, pain, and sorrow. The worst nightmare comes to life in the limelight of envy. Patience is a virtue, and the product of failure can be a success. Talents are in your writing; your hands could be someone's blessing. Never had the upmost respect for myself, as a woman I looked past my beauty. I didn't even know what beautiful meant, but I knew what ugly was! It doesn't take much to become that. Looking in the mirror of damaged goods walking the universe alone. The light that reflected from me showcased my errors.

Sagittarius Fire

Ashamed from the toxic turmoil she was involved in caused her to overthink what love could be. The desire for pure passion burned in her soul like hot coils. The thought of being touched by another person stung like a scorpion. Over processing the grief of separation, her pillow was like a bucket catching the tears that fell every night from the silence of her weakness. Who is she? The walking woman of Bama blues. Her bosom is filled with insecurities. Trying to uplift herself she found comfort in mother nature. A lifetime of hard work slowly became suffocating with no financial gain. As a child she thought like a child but as she grew older, she put away childish things. Growing to know herself she walked with bold confidence. She rose from the ashes of the burning romance sensation. The fetal stage of one's heartbeat blossoming in the moonlight of water silhouette.

Bama love

I loved you from the beginning of time. My silence got in the way of who I could trust. I often asked myself, can I believe and hold on to every word you said? Through you, I found out that real love was hard to find. Your love couldn't be more counterfeit than the love that already broke me. How hard can it be to hold your head up high even though being good enough is never good enough? Love is like a water fountain. Giving a clean appearance but bitter to taste. This divine woman came into her own character of loving herself fearlessly. It's not my fault that I wasn't loved correctly but I will forever apologize to myself for allowing their hurt to love me. I couldn't be the woman for you because I had to be the woman for me. Bama love.

Spoiled love

Forbidden love only comes a dime and dozens. The love that I once truly desired wasn't the love that I needed. I saw real love from others one too many times in plain view. Only to be hijacked by true love for myself. Trying to right your wrongs for true love is tough while also finding out it's just too damn late. Maybe that's something you didn't need in your lifetime of happiness. I forgave you to try to save you and myself. The very thought of forgetting the memories that we shared made me sick. I was always on the receiving end of forbidden love.

Past

Your Past Is One Thing That Can Lead You To A Lifetime Of Regret. Just Being Cold Hearted Will Make You Stop Living Your Life. You Have To Forgive Yourself For Holding On To The Sorrow and Shame. The Things Accumulated Over The Years Built Up On The Inside. Circumstances and Situations That Belittled Me To The Point Of No Return, Became Filthy Over Time. I Couldn't Speak For Not Knowing If You Would Or Wouldn't Accept Me. I Sit There Looking In Your Eyes And I Had To Turn Away. I Wasn't Woman Enough To The Core. I Watched You Grow Beautifully Like A Worm Growing Into A Beautiful Butterfly. The Ugly Worm That Was Ever Born Into This Universe of Heaven and Hell. The Cocoon That Stay Hideaway Through Her Shadow of Darkness Knowing I Didn't Have Anything To Offer But Misery. I Couldn't Destroy Your Life of Happiness That Is How Much I Love You and Always Will.

Blessed and Cursed

Throughout my life, I questioned love, the heartstring of heartaches, the extended root on a tree, every twist and turn, the curves flexible with the drop of every heartbeat, the silent words that turn into action of endurance. I will always carry you in my heart. The ship never stopped sailing. It takes one time for the heart to split in two. The ship is sailing through the blood vessel between the broken heart. The curse of how I could even hate myself, loving the most precious baby that came through the birth canal. I want your world to be filled with the warmth happiness brings. Consequently, it only got filled with bloodshed of teardrops. I blame myself for what I could have done differently. Why does love hurt so bad and cause history to repeat itself? Shattered like glass only to see myself within the faded pieces of life's transformation.

Beautiful Smile

I wish I could see your face again, especially that beautiful smile. I know we're distant right now. I'm in one state and you're in another. When I go to sleep at night, I dream that we're close excluding the distance. I visit the landmark, bringing back memories of how we first met. I remember when I first laid eyes on you. At that moment, I knew my life was going to change forever. You were day, and I was night. We couldn't get enough of each other; we would always be together. I was the fire; you were my water trying to cool me off. We couldn't keep our hands off of each other. A moment that didn't last a lifetime was like an hourglass with time running out. I fell hard, but all good things come to an end. What I admire is your strength compared to my weakness, pride, confidence, security, stability, communication, and commitment. You were the total package that completed me. I didn't block your blessing by allowing you to heal me.

Alabama No More

My childhood was demolished from the face of this earth no more life, laugh, or love. My world came crashing down without evidence that it could get better. No more family meals around the dinner table. No more helping me with my homework. No more family pictures. No more family trips to the country. A home that was destroyed by a disastrous and tragic event on a sweet summer night. My childhood friend vanished. I carry the weight in my eyes with sorrow and despair. I will never hear I love you. It's one thing to fight for your country, and it's another thing to die for your country. The police didn't believe that the truth could come from a child. I knew then I would be overlooked, unsuccessful, and belittled. I already prepared myself for the worst. How could I ever imagine my life without the one I love. The ocean without the water. The sky without the birds. The trees without the leaves. The daddy issues I had led me to begin looking for love in all the wrong places. I Wanted somebody, honestly anybody, to love me and I couldn't even love myself.

Then all of a sudden I had finally gave in and loved myself.

Ashamed

Ashamed

I found myself looking at old pictures of myself.

Ashamed

wondering if I was ever beautiful

Ashamed

of my insecurities and lack of self-confidence.

Ashamed

of the choices I made, but

I needed to learn the lesson.

Ashamed,

I can never do anything right.

Ashamed

of myself as a woman, not a woman of beauty

Ashamed

 embarrassed by the guilt of not speaking my mind.

 Ashamed

of holding on to words in my heart.

Ashamed

Once I pour these words from my heart, are you going

to listen?

Ashamed

of my anger building up over time.

Ashamed of who I am and what I have become.

Ashamed

of the disappointment. I'm trying to make me a better person each and every day. I can't do anything else but try.

Grandmother

In the midst of the storm, you and my aunt came to Alabama to rescue me. I was on the ground, just a vine of hurt and pain. You came and picked me up like a berry off of a tree stuck in a brush along the vineyard getting overlooked. It saddened my heart to leave Alabama on a greyhound bus. It smelled of old cheese and work boots. I appreciate you for not giving up on me. Believing in me when I didn't believe in myself until your dying day. I talked to you and my aunt about everything until you left this earth. How can I sit here and hate South Carolina? My grandmother gave me life. I am glad you were showing me the way towards a new opportunity. I know I am not alone, and I will always have a grandmother to reflect back on. You accepted me as I was. I had to learn how to accept myself on many occasions through the good and not so good. Thank you for the lesson of perseverance. It became a blessing as time went on.

Farewell Forever

Columbia introduced itself without saying a word and gave me a name that wasn't important for the time being. The uniqueness of your namesake and the story was unfolding right before my eyes. The moment of being belittled happened sooner than expected. I imagined not hearing your voice. I imagined not holding you in my arms anymore. I imagined the smile on your face. I imagined the walk of confidence you had. I imagined the laughs we shared together. I imagined your words of encouragement that melted my heart. I couldn't have imagined you not being here anymore. Goodbye is hard to say so I'll just say, farewell forever.

Empowerment

Empowerment is just a word with many definitions that we come across on the daily basics. The shades of color, shape, and size from our hair texture to our eyes to our bones structure are all different. The lessons that are beneficial; fulfilling your purpose is your biggest blessing. Crown jewels of diamond and emerald that captivated the challenge of our imperfection. The burden of life weighs on your shoulders. Life is like the rose buds of many colorful rose petals that are beautiful, gorgeous, amazing, wonderful, and extraordinary no matter what comes your way. You're unique in your own special way or you wouldn't have become the person that you are today. Our character goes a long way in life. Happiness comes within adding value to your life's accomplishments.

Heart of heart

Love is a beautiful ray of light that reflects self-love. She ran away from herself, ditching self-love. She fell in love with not loving herself. While running away from self-love, she slowly began to understand why it's important to love yourself. It has been a long time since she admitted that she never really loved herself. She is me; I am her. When you see the life, you were entitled to, it's hard seeing everything wrong and not according to what you expected. Step one: It is time to lift the burden of not loving yourself off your shoulders. Step two: see your life as just the beginning. A new day is a day of new opportunities. Change your mindset and open your mind to change. If it didn't work for you in the beginning it's okay because everything works for your good.

Live

Do you live to keep or do you live to let go?
A man goes through a lot and keeps lots of things on the inside, one heartbeat at a time. Once they tell those emotions it hurts them to the core. This is the reason why they hold on to secrets, but everything isn't a secret. I know I don't get everything right myself, but men are different treasures. Yes, we all have our problems day in and day out. Men need somebody to uplift them as well on a daily basis. Stop getting mad at simple things, making something out of nothing. They need some words of encouragement throughout the day. They changed their lives for the better, so don't criticize. The men are the seed carriers of your precious babies. You will see the fruit of your labor if you keep your eyes open. It's not all their fault that they go through things. If they help you grow you help them. No matter how long you've been on this journey you've become your own identity. Men, I believe in you and I'm proud of you. One love Bama Style.

Give Credit Where It's Due

Apparently, we all know we can't accomplish anything on our own without the necessary tools, networking and taking accountability for our actions. Who are the people surrounding you holding the ladder for you to climb to the top? Do you think your gifts and talents are yours because you're you? No, somebody prayed for you the 9 months that you were in your mother's womb. More consistently for God's will to be done before the seed was ever planted. So, with all due respect, tell somebody today "I appreciate you and without you there would be no me". The lessons that were taught carried the weight of encouragement to help you become a better person. Seeing your lifestyle for once and making the appropriate change says a lot about oneself as a human being. Why stay stuck in a cycle of grief when you can make the necessary changes to become better. For example, my father was holding the ladder for me to put Christmas lights on the house. Knowing me, I kept looking down. Thinking I was going to fall, he said, "Why do you keep looking down?

Look up! If you keep looking back you're going to miss what is in front of your face". How do you know where you are going if you look back. Don't look on the side either. If you fall, I will always be here to catch you. I already caught you. Don't forget the lessons of the past. Those are lifetime lessons that will help you in your future endeavors.

Mother

I miss how the words came together forming a sentence that rolled off your tongue so smoothly. I miss your face. It was as soft as cocoa butter and as brown as a pecan. Your voice of concern never showed fear. I miss your eyes that pierced through my soul. You let me grow and go and allowed me to come back with a burden or two. The expression of your word willpower dedicated the memories of not forgetting where you came from. In the limelight, all on your own timing, if you move fast or slow, you're exactly where you're supposed to be. Don't ever look at what you don't have, look at what you do have and the lessons that carried you through. The rose petals of love, mercy, and grace. Graced with gratitude. Appreciate everybody that consistently comes into your world, they may have a lesson you still need to learn, my child. Bama/Metro one love 🖤

I love you

I love you; I'll always love you. A heart is like a desert burning with pain of discomfort. A heart that was cold on ice frozen like Antarctica, with a big glacier of snow to the core of regret. I fell in love with the story that your eyes told, your hands felt like a teddy bear that gave comfort. We're both on this journey to grow while being a part. I couldn't show you that I wanted to stick around so I did what I do best....HIDE. Love is like a tree; it runs deep rooted by feelings. Love extends like branches so far that it feels like it can touch your soul. Finding a new way to conquer this world alone feels like sandpaper scrapping my eyeball. It took a village to help me overcome this new life alone. The Berry village made it easy for me to express my emotions without rebuke. Learning how to deal with the struggle is learning how to survive. My heart was made whole again through smiles from those who loved me. The healing aspect of having a healthy heart 💜 I'm still a work in progress and it doesn't matter how fast or slow it takes as long as I stay the course. Time is the essence and distance is time. I LOVE YOU.

Acknowledgements

I've dedicated this book of poems to my children Reaqwon Garrick, and The Fighter 4 Maurice, Elijah, Jeremiah and Joshua. Lastly, to my siblings Sally and Samuel Berry.

As you read the different poems, always remember to love those connected to you. Life is like steam, one second, it's here the next it's gone. Kind words can go a long way, so spread them every chance you get.

-Mom

www.ingramcontent.com/pod-product-compliance
Lightning Source LLC
Chambersburg PA
CBHW060358130626
46553CB00003B/1290